Psaiku

Haiku of the Psyche

Robert Meyers-Lussier

Writers Club Press
New York   Lincoln   Shanghai

**Psaiku
Haiku of the Psyche**

All Rights Reserved © 2001 by Robert Meyers-Lussier

No part of this book may be reproduced or transmitted in any form or by any means, graphic, electronic, or mechanical, including photocopying, recording, taping, or by any information storage retrieval system, without the permission in writing from the publisher.

Writers Club Press
an imprint of iUniverse, Inc.

For information address:
iUniverse, Inc.
2021 Pine Lake Road, Suite 100
Lincoln, NE 68512
www.iuniverse.com

ISBN: 0-595-21161-5 (Pbk)
ISBN: 0-595-75285-3 (Cloth)

Printed in the United States of America

Dedicated to my Mom—Diana, and my Dad—Robert Sr. I owe all with which I have been blessed to you both.

Acknowledgements

To Ron Partridge—You were the one person responsible for providing me the opportunity to begin writing Psaiku, and getting it published (via the web). Without you, this body of work would not exist.

To my friends on IRC, too numerous to mention them all—It was on IRC, over a couple of nights, just fooling around with some old Haiku I had written, that the encouragement, and eventual meeting of Ron (see above), got me started writing. Thank you to all of you, and please, keep chatting!
:-)

To my Mother (and Duffy)—For putting up with me; all my faults and foibles; and for standing by me, and my work. Someday, you guys, it will all have been worth it! I love you!

To Dorothy Pence—Who I will forever thank; for being the one person in this world who filled me with enough confidence to continue writing at my earliest stages of development.

To Maravonda (now defunct) and Jitters—It is so important for me to have a comfortable place to write, and these havens of comfort (aka coffeehouses) provided a perfect environment. And thank goodness for iced Americanos!

To all my friends who love poetry—Kathleen Blatz, John Holahan, Tom and Sally Haase, Susan and Harvey Peck, Dean and Susan Barkley, Greg

Psaiku

and Kelly Waltigney, Colleen Dickmann, Anne McCullough, Christine Chalstrom, Kay Eiseman and any and all who I may have forgotten. Although I may lose contact, you will always have a place in my heart regards this body of work.

To Sue (my sister), her family, and Tony (my brother), and his family—Just for being who you are in my life!

To my Dad—I love you.

To each person(s) whose actions inspired every poem in this book, excepting my own. You have helped make me who I am today—for better or for worse...

Preface

It's funny. I began writing these poems in response to a challenge; an online challenge from someone I had met on the internet, on Internet Relay Chat (IRC), to be more specific. What has resulted is a recounting of a five year adventure!

As a child, I reveled in the simplicity of Haiku, tasty morsels of the English language that nearly anyone could grasp, and perhaps even write. Haiku are not American, not even English. They are an original product of the Japanese, but what masters of simplicity they are! Three lines; five syllables—seven syllables—five syllables, and that's it. Haiku, as the Japanese have represented it, focus on nature. The observation of nature, and thus man's relationship to it, has been mastered. Subtle, beautiful, picaresque. In Japanese they are especially lovely.

What about the observation of man, within his surroundings? What about the inner struggles of man? What about the relationship between men? Cannot there also be beauty in brief representations of man's nature? Although I have written in many formats, particularly longer free-form poems, and as a reporter, I have found the most satisfaction in choosing 18—25 words to represent a feeling, an emotion, an observation. To be able to squeeze out of our miraculous lexicon a most complete thought, or hope, or even story, in so few words or syllables, has gone well beyond simply being a challenge. It has become a new form of expression. A Psaiku, if you will, or Haiku of the psyche.

Psaiku

In 1996, not but a week before I wrote the first poem here, I met a man online in an IRC channel who enjoyed Haiku I had written some time earlier. He wished to learn and perfect this art form, so he issued me a challenge. If I would write two Haiku a week, he would write two, then he would post them on a web site he designed. As people came to the site, they would then vote for the Haiku they liked best. Over three or four months of this, I realized what had occurred: I was no longer writing Haiku. I was focusing on my life, on what and/or who surrounded me, my mind, concerns, relations, etc. I had also accumulated a sizeable amount of very unique poems. Later, perhaps a year after writing these poems, I came to discover that something miraculous had occurred. While I was no longer the same man who began writing, I had documented this most difficult year (or so) of transition of my life with this unique form of expression.

* * *

Life is not static, and neither is this work! I have added a primer for those who might wish to expand on the psaiku concept, as well as two poems. I would also like to encourage you to visit my website—www.bobmeyers.com, where you can delve into a bit more of what has made, and continues to make me, well…me!

—-10 October 2003—-

Psaiku Primer

I. The structure remains similar to haiku. Three lines. *It's mandatory.*

II. There are no less than 5-7-5 syllables, which is based on the haiku model. *It's also mandatory.*

III. The rhythm is meter. Since we don't speak in syllables, I contemplate the meter of each line. Thus there is no set number of syllables, although I consider the flow of our language. I am not bound to it, but I am aware of it. Consider the following poem from the book:

Beauty and beholder
Eye of newt and bestial lover
Early grave dug shallow

Has the following rhythm (a '\' represents the stressed syllable):

\ u \ u \ u
\ u \ u \ u \ u
\ u \ u \ u

The rhythm of the first and third lines begin stressed, whereas the second line begins unstressed, or vice-versa.

Psaiku

IV. Line two must always be at least one syllable longer than the first and third lines. Natural language would dictate at least two syllables (or more pairs), but it is not mandatory. An idea/emotion/observation still has to be fully conveyed. If you were to gauge every poem in the book, you would find the meters/counts are all over the place. It may be 5-7-5, 5-8-6, 6-10-6, etc.

V. Subject matter must deal with us humans. Not nature, as the Japanese have been doing for centuries. It could be an emotion, or an emotional state. It could be about some experience. It could be about some observation, of yourself, another person, or a society. It could be about an abstract, such as death, or evil, or good. *This too is mandatory.*

VI. Be creative! There are so very many ways to manipulate the English language, it's a hoot! We have homonyms, synonyms, repetition, hyperbole, etc.—all that fun stuff you may have studied.

Within our mind's eye

The pristine soul of nature

Sees with clarity

—-12 July 1996—-

Robert Meyers-Lussier

Aural waves of notes

Wash away the grit of time

Gaia's song restored

—-*17 July 1996*—-

Robert Meyers-Lussier

Summer's hand stroking

Bronzed hides of taut effigies

Sacrificial lambs

—-17 July 1996—-

Robert Meyers-Lussier

Levi'd soul of love

Taut, bronzed body cotton-sheathed

Carnivore's delight!

—-17 July 1996—-

Robert Meyers-Lussier

Playful petunias

Kiss my nose with petulance

Scents of life empowered

—-18 July 1996—-

Robert Meyers-Lussier

I

Monolithic spires
Sway in rhythmic unison
Field of fragrant dreams

II

Field of fragrant dreams
Technicolor hopes renewed
Eden's love yet blooms

III

Eden's love yet blooms
In snake infested orchards
Red delicious tears

—-24 July 1996—-

Robert Meyers-Lussier

Natural rhythms

Predetermined preferences

DNA divined

—-*24 July 1996*—-

Robert Meyers-Lussier

A glance skewed by time

An embrace frozen in time

Love will come with time

—-*24 July 1996*—-

Robert Meyers-Lussier

Amphibious minds
Camouflaged amongst the weeds
Muskrat's midnight snack

—-30 July 1996—-

Robert Meyers-Lussier

Solitary loon

The voice of Christ embodied

Liquid crucifix

—-31 July 1996—-

Robert Meyers-Lussier

Magnetic dew drops

Compel earth and sky to meet

Blessed is the morn!

—-*31 July 1996*—-

Robert Meyers-Lussier

Naked is the day
Where cognizance slumbers soundly
And ignorance awakes

—-31 July 1996—-

Robert Meyers-Lussier

Tissue paper skin

Easily torn and seen through

Crumpled egos tossed

—-5 August 1996—-

Robert Meyers-Lussier

Corn-fed gluttony

Readies the beast for slaughter

Pig of hate consumed

—-5 August 1996—-

Robert Meyers-Lussier

Sleeping giants lie
On Lilliputian beaches
Dwarfed by prejudice

—-*7 August 1996*—-

Robert Meyers-Lussier

Tribes of Earth rejoice!

As raindrops joined make oceans

So too minds of men

—-9 August 1996—-

Robert Meyers-Lussier

Hummingbird's liqueur

Nectar-laden fleur-de-lis

Aphrodisiac

—-9 August 1996—-

Robert Meyers-Lussier

Healers of this Earth
Johnny Appleseeds of hope
Planting trees of life

—-15 August 1996—-

Robert Meyers-Lussier

Green-eyed samurai
Sun-adorned chrysanthemum
Buddha's pride and joy

—-22 August 1996—-

Robert Meyers-Lussier

Haters of this life

Gaze into your god's abyss

Reap your just rewards

—-*22 August 1996*—-

Robert Meyers-Lussier

Digital caress

Electrifies my belly

Heart and soul recharged

—-3 September 1996—-

Robert Meyers-Lussier

Grinding synergy

Intoxicating rhythms

Fantasies conspired

—-*18 September 1996*—-

Robert Meyers-Lussier

I

Hot and sweet your breath
Swirls around lips softly pressed
Against my yielding neck

II

Despite lascivious beginnings
I feel the pain your soul endures
I see the smile inside your heart

III

Family matters
Divorce and child custody
Why can't life be fair?

Psaiku

IV

Temporal visions
Of passionate embraces
Instantly denied

V

Hope beyond all hopes
I pray for your happiness
Can we please be friends?

—-25 September 1996—-

Robert Meyers-Lussier

I drink from your skin
Cappuccino'd nourishment
Caffeine laced delights!

—-17 October 1996—-

Milk and honey smile
Sweetens simply my existence
Lightening my soul

—-21 October 1996—-

Off this speeding train
Into cesspools of routine
Jumps bared your shallow soul

—-26 November 1996—-

Robert Meyers-Lussier

Supreme Voyage

Billowing white sails
Fill with winds Themis-conspired
As storm brews overhead

* * *

An Ark of Hope buoyed
On oceans of tears cleansing
This Earth soiled by sin

* * *

Captain at the helm
Her hand steady, her mind clear
Voyage of the soul

* * *

White light splits the sky
Impending doom forged by sorrow
Zeus' anger thunders

Psaiku

* * *

Three daughters spinning
Thread seven gifts of counsel
As heaven's temper flares

* * *

Rocked by saline mountains
Skipper battens down her hatches
Occupants secured

* * *

Seven animals
Bear witness special qualities
When summed complete the whole

* * *

Justice will prevail
If each these parts do lessons learn
This voyage of the soul

Robert Meyers-Lussier

The Lamb

Sweet and gentle lamb
Free from hate and pure of heart
Unclouded innocence

The Dolphin

Sonic melodies
Dolphin sung in murky depths
Crystal clear its voice

The Dove

Airborne elegance
Breaks free the reigns of earthly woes
Dove's mission peace driven

Psaiku

The Donkey

Upon its back packed
Heavy burdens human borne
Donkey's grace in service

The Owl

Artemis familiar
Predatory bird of knowledge
Owl sight all-seeing

The Loon

Cacophonous Earth
Loon lullabies do haunting join
Distinct its contribution

Robert Meyers-Lussier

The Dog

Human-kind in need
Instinctively compassionate
Lays down the dog its life

—-4 November 1996—-

Robert Meyers-Lussier

Sugar plum engines
Dance in Mercedes Benz dreams
Fairy tale fantasies

—-*19 December 1996*—-

Robert Meyers-Lussier

Percussion plundered
Drum's skin stretched taut, yet yielding
Why must cymbals clash?

—-*22 December 1996*—-

Robert Meyers-Lussier

Sincere melodies

Hummed to a requiem beat

Mozart's reminiscings

—-*27 December 1996*—-

Robert Meyers-Lussier

Panther-skinned beings

Hunt not by instinct alone

Cunning's kill is swift

—-1 January 1997—-

Robert Meyers-Lussier

Coffeehouse spirit

Liquored-up poltergeist struggling

Living post-mortem dreams

—-*13 January 1997*—-

Robert Meyers-Lussier

Schoolboy hopes and dreams
Inhabit ancient carcasses
Rotting from within

—-16 January 1997—-

Robert Meyers-Lussier

Keyboard kisses foreplayed

Meeting is such sweet sorrow

"Can't we just be friends?"

—-*16 January 1997*—-

Robert Meyers-Lussier

Toasted paradigms

Buttered with stainless steel lies

Jam on shifting morals

—-24 January 1997—-

Robert Meyers-Lussier

Life's raw pure essence
Triangulated energies
Soul-drenched joie-de-vivre

—-29 January 1997—-

Robert Meyers-Lussier

Random acts of kindness
Pandora's gift reciprocated
Free will vindicated

—-30 January 1997—-

Robert Meyers-Lussier

Glowing from within
Your beauty shines as points of light
Tanning my existence

—-30 January 1997—-

Robert Meyers-Lussier

Saline destiny

Awash in impure mystery

Reverse osmosis screams

—-11 February 1997—-

Robert Meyers-Lussier

Father Time in drag
Sequined in history's baubles
A queen's prerogative

—-*18 February 1997*—-

Robert Meyers-Lussier

Wildfires rage within

Charred surfaces glisten seductively

Moths to a flame captured

—-*23 February 1997*—-

Robert Meyers-Lussier

Twisted cones of fate

Vanilla paths and chocolate detours

Homogenized frozen treats

—-8 March 1997—-

Robert Meyers-Lussier

Giant apples peeled
Innocence peeled and quartered
Baked in decadence

—-18 March 1997—-

Robert Meyers-Lussier

Brainerd beleaguered
Endings outnumber beginnings
Night is closing in

✶ ✶ ✶

Into darkness comes light
Trapped, your soul brightens stagnant minds
Anticipating nothing

—-5 April 1997—-

Robert Meyers-Lussier

Twin bite marks inflicted
Infect me with immortal visions
Of lascivious perfection

—-*23 April 1997*—-

Robert Meyers-Lussier

Forged metal kisses
Pierce my virgin soul unknowing
Unexpected pain

—-4 May 1997—-

Tumultuous pain
Wretched aortal contusions
Fireworks rage within

—-23 April 1997—-

Sweet, delicious pain
Juice from fruits forbidden nourishing
Encouraging new growth

—-23 May 1997—-

Robert Meyers-Lussier

My nose a strawberry

Your teeth white rabbits nibbling

Feeding on my desires

—-15 May 1997—-

Robert Meyers-Lussier

Unexpected visits
Impetuous moments spurred
By pandoric inhibitions

—-18 July 1997—-

Robert Meyers-Lussier

Incestuous pain

Bites the hand that feeds my soul

Love's hunger never ceases

—-20 July 1997—-

Robert Meyers-Lussier

Corrugated lust

Flimsy box of love debauched

Packaged for consumption

—-*17 August 1997*—-

Robert Meyers-Lussier

Uncertain attractions
Youth-induced aesthetic desires
Playground of delusions

—-*9 September 1997*—-

Furtive glances stolen
From boys who look the other way
Childhood highway robbers

Congratulatory jeers
Celebrate self-discovery
Humiliating victory

Psaiku

Derision divides me
Fear permeates my existence
Secret are my longings

Suspicions abound
Hateful epitaphs slice through me
My chain mail weak-linked lies

Crushed velvet blackness
Cloaks blanched remains skeletally bound
Closets are for freaks

—-10 September 1997—-

Robert Meyers-Lussier

Hedonism rules

In pleasure's palace my soul resides

Evicted from normality

—-*28 September 1997*—-

Robert Meyers-Lussier

Roman emissaries
Twelve souls immortal hand-delivered
Faces of impending doom

—-*28 September 1997*—-

Robert Meyers-Lussier

Petals folded tightly

Gilded buds of masculinity

Await celestial rains

—-24 June 1998—-

Robert Meyers-Lussier

Once in a lifetime

A rose blooms unlike any other

My soul has touched its glory

—-22 July 1998—-

Robert Meyers-Lussier

A kiss is just a kiss

Without love's poisoned arrow transfixed

Four lips do meet, then part

—-*27 July 1998*—-

Robert Meyers-Lussier

I hear within your gaze

The smell of Moorish whispers famished

Beguiled sentience mystified

—-27 July 1998—-

Robert Meyers-Lussier

Sugar-coated silence

Placebo for hope easily ingested

Decays my enameled spirit

—-*28 July 1998*—-

Robert Meyers-Lussier

Naïve zealousness

Double-edged sword of innocence

Camelot revisited

—-*28 July 1998*—-

Robert Meyers-Lussier

Venus fly-trap baited

A lion's den draped in jeans and a tank

Entrapment by delusion

—-3 August 1998—-

Robert Meyers-Lussier

Remorseful conscience scammed

Heinous aberration of trust

Pastoral devastation

—-3 August 1998—-

Robert Meyers-Lussier

Distant shores obscured

Your heart I see as plain as day

Your touch ethereal

—-7 October 1998—-

Robert Meyers-Lussier

A dream in living color

My nightmares erased by laughter and smiles

I pray my slumber endures

—-*10 October 1998*—-

Robert Meyers-Lussier

Bewitching trinity
Three souls embroiled in celestial intrigue
Mortality's pains withstood

—-*14 October 1998*—-

Robert Meyers-Lussier

Peanut butter exploits
Snoopy muskrat in search of love
Unmitigated blockhead

—-17 October 1998—-

Robert Meyers-Lussier

Beauty and beholder

Eye of newt and bestial lover

Early grave dug shallow

—-*13 January 1999*—-

Robert Meyers-Lussier

Obesity and closets
Twin pyres of self-doubt loathing
Purging hopes and dreams

Thin and out and seized with visions
Singed with age a phoenix risen
Redemption mitigated

—-13 February 1999—-

Robert Meyers-Lussier

Three dimensions conspiring
Temporal treason your presence commits
Compromising the fourth

—-*25 February 1999*—-

Robert Meyers-Lussier

Ignorance is bliss

On brilliant worlds a lone mind blinded

Safety in delusion

—-*26 February 1999*—-

Robert Meyers-Lussier

Corporeal loyalty
Boldly embraces another man's soul
When masculine in form

When feminine in form
Bejeweled and set atop her ideals
Loyalty's shadow morphs

—-27 February 1999—-

Robert Meyers-Lussier

Youth engorged syringes
Satiate love-starved junkie veins
Tracks of emptiness

Reality fading
Tripped-out pubescence resuscitated
Cerebral ecstasy

—-2 March 1999—-

Withdrawal my heart kissing
Seizures lick my body with pleasure
Addiction's oral fix fixed

—-3 March 1999—-

Robert Meyers-Lussier

Four walls and a roof
Human experience sheltered
Solid glass constructed

—-16 March 1999—-

Robert Meyers-Lussier

Ethnic grit clinging

To filthy souls penned in by history

Bloody bath drawn cleansing

—-6 April 1999—-

Robert Meyers-Lussier

Ignorant pretender

Self-loathing clothed in flannels and caps

The emperor's new haute couture

—-11 April 1999—-

Robert Meyers-Lussier

A blizzard of free will

Frozen crystals of divine rights blowing

Settle on sinners drifting

—-*16 April 1999*—-

Robert Meyers-Lussier

Invading viral armies

Rape and pillage this soul's temple

Fate's forged passage ambushed

—-16 January 2000—-

Robert Meyers-Lussier

Sophisticated dodo
Flightless bird with social standing
Darwinism justified

—-*29 May 2000*—-

Robert Meyers-Lussier

Canine constellation

Queen in a kingdom of stars

Night's best friend holds court

—-*13 November 2001*—-

Robert Meyers-Lussier

Lust-induced mirages

Digital oases in a desert of love

Harem of caravanned fools

—-*23 May 2002*—-

Robert Meyers-Lussier

On clouds of confusion floating

Spin frisbee dreams tossed from closet doors folded

Foggy friendships dissipating

—-3 July 2002—-

0-595-21161-5

NORMANDALE COMMUNITY COLLEGE
LIBRARY
9700 FRANCE AVENUE SOUTH
BLOOMINGTON, MN 55431-4399

Printed in the United States
28029LVS00006B/103